FLAVORS OF THE WORLD

THE FOOD OF ITALY

Sara Louise Kras

Marshall Cavendish
Benchmark
New York

Published by Marshall Cavendish Benchmark

An imprint of Marshall Cavendish Corporation

Website: www.marshallcavendish.us

Other Marshall Cavendish Offices:

Marshall Cavendish International (Asia) Private Limited, 1 New Industrial Road, Singapore 536196 • Marshall Cavendish International (Thailand) Co Ltd. 253 Asoke, 12th Flr, Sukhumvit 21 Road, Klongtoey Nua, Wattana, Bangkok 10110, Thailand • Marshall Cavendish (Malaysia) Sdn Bhd, Times Subang, Lot 46, Subang Hi-Tech Industrial Park, Batu Tiga, 40000 Shah Alam, Selangor Darul Ehsan, Malaysia

Marshall Cavendish is a trademark of Times Publishing Limited

All websites were available and accurate when this book was sent to press.

Library of Congress Cataloging-in-Publication Data
Kras, Sara Louise.
The food of Italy / Sara Louise Kras.
    p. cm. — (Flavors of the world)
Includes bibliographical references and index.
Summary: "Explores the culture, traditions, and festivals of Italy through its food"—Provided by publisher.
ISBN 978-1-60870-236-7 (print) ISBN 978-1-60870-689-1 (ebook)
    1. Food habits—Italy. 2. Festivals—Italy. 3. Italy—Social life and customs. I. Title.
    GT2853.I8K73 2012
394.1'20945—dc22
2010021542

Editor: Christine Florie
Publisher: Michelle Bisson
Art Director: Anahid Hamparian
Series Designer: Kay Petronio

Expert Reader: Fabio Parasecoli, The New School, Associate Professor and Coordinator of Food Studies, New York, NY

Photo research by Marybeth Kavanagh

Cover photo by David Kleyn/Alamy

The photographs in this book are used by permission and through the courtesy of: *SuperStock:* Axiom Photographic Limited, 4; Photononstop, 8; Terry Harris PCL, 9; age fotostock, 11, 24, 38; Transtock, 13; Silvio Fiore, 16; Food and Drink, 22, 28, 37; Axiom Photographic Limited, 27; Hemis.fr, 34, 46, 57; Robert Harding Picture Library, 29; Westend61, 40; Angelo Cavalli, 47; Photocuisine, 54; *Photolibrary:* Federico Meneghetti, 7; *Corbis:* Stephanie Maze, 10; *Art Resource, NY:* Scala, 14; *age fotostock:* Marco Andras, 20; *Alamy:* John Ferro Sims, 21; CuboImages srl, 26; Tony French, 33; Luciano Mortula, 41; First Light, 51; *The Image Works:* Ethel Wolvovitz, 42; *Getty Images:* Annabelle Breakey/The Image Bank, 55; *Fotolia:* Volff (olive), covers, 1, 64; Akhilesh Sharma (banner), cover, 1, 3, 5, 17, 31, 43, 53; Photka (garlic), 3; Sandra Cunningham (spices) 8, 20, 41, 45, 54; *Shutterstock:* Suto Norbert Zsolt (map), cover, 1, 2-3, 23, 28, 30, 37, 40; *VectorStock:* Nicemonkey (plate), back cover, 3

Maps (pp. 6 & 18) by Mapping Specialists Limited

Printed in Malaysia (T)

135642

CONTENTS

Welcome to Italy

Italy is famous for its food. Italians claim that they taught the rest of Europe how to cook and eat. Today, Italian dishes such as pizza and spaghetti are enjoyed the world over. But Italy's contributions to the art of cooking also include such well-known ingredients as olive oil, tomato sauce, and Parmesan cheese.

Seas, Mountains, and Volcanoes

Italy, located in southern Europe, is a large peninsula extending into the Mediterranean Sea. The country is in the shape of a boot. Two and one-half miles off the "boot tip" is the island of Sicily. Other famous Italian islands are Sardinia and Capri, and there are several **archipelagos**, as well.

Four seas, which are arms of the Mediterranean Sea, border Italy. The Ligurian Sea is off the northwest coast. Further south, the Tyrrhenian Sea borders the west coast and the islands of Sardinia and Sicily. The southernmost sea is the Ionian Sea.

The fields of Tuscany provide the perfect location to picnic on the flavorful foods of Italy.

TOPOGRAPHICAL MAP OF ITALY

ALPS

DOLOMITE MOUNTAINS

PO VALLEY

APENNINES

Ligurian Sea

ITALY

Adriatic Sea

★ Rome

Mt. Vesuvius

Capri

Sardinia

Tyrrhenian Sea

Ionian Sea

Sicily

Mt. Etna

Mediterranean Sea

Finally, separating Italy from the Balkan country of Croatia is the Adriatic Sea.

Northern Italy is defined by the Alps, the largest mountain range in Europe. The majestic Dolomite Mountains located in northeastern Italy are part of the Alps. Jagged snow peaks form the crest of the Dolomites, and their natural beauty is awe inspiring. Visitors ski the slopes during winter and hike there in the summer. Because this Alpine region is cooler than much of the rest of Italy, hearty food such as thick stews and pork dishes are popular, as well as sauces prepared with butter and cream.

The Po River flows through the Po Valley, Italy's largest plain. Huge fields of sweet corn and rice grow in this extremely fertile, well-watered region of north-central Italy.

Emilia-Romagna lies in the Po Valley, a region of fertile plains rich with crops of corn and rice.

Classic Risotto

Italians make a dish called risotto from short-grain rice, which is high in starch and can absorb large amounts of liquid. Sometimes served instead of pasta, risotto is creamy and can be mixed with vegetables, cheese, sausage, or seafood. An adult should help in preparing and cooking this dish.

Ingredients

Olive oil

Half an onion, minced

1 tablespoon minced garlic

1 cup uncooked short-grain rice, such as Arborio

3 1/2 cups chicken broth

1 tablespoon grated Parmesan cheese

Salt and pepper

Directions

Cover the bottom of a pan with olive oil and heat until hot. Cook the onion until soft. Add the garlic and rice and cook for 2 minutes, stirring. Add 1/2 cup of the broth and cook until the broth is gone.

Add the remaining broth, a half-cup at a time, stirring until broth is absorbed. Cook until the rice is creamy and soft but slightly crisp in the center. Add cheese and salt and pepper to taste.

South of the Po Valley are the Apennine Mountains, sometimes referred to as the backbone of Italy. Because these mountains, which stretch down through central Italy, are not as high as the Alps, sheep and goats graze on grass along their rolling slopes. Lamb is a local specialty and is served often. Truffles grow beneath the ground of the Apennine forests. These small plants, with a taste similar to that of mushrooms, are considered to be a delicacy and are sparingly added to provide a unique flavor to dishes.

Hunting for Truffles

About the size of a golf ball, truffles often have a hard, black bumpy skin. Since they grow underground and are hard to find, they are very expensive. Truffles are found below the roots of various trees such as oak and beech, but finding them can be tricky. Specially trained dogs are used to search out the truffles by detecting their strong smell. Once located, the truffles are dug up and sold.

Not only does Italy have mountains, it also has several volcanoes, both active and extinct. Mount Etna, the most active volcano in Europe, is located on Sicily. Another famous volcano, Mount Vesuvius, lies just outside the southern city of Naples. In 79 CE Vesuvius erupted, wiping out the town of Pompeii. Its most recent eruption was in 1944.

Sharing meals is an important part of Italian culture.

Culture

The family is the most important unit in Italian culture. Children often live at home until they marry. Grandparents sometimes live with the family, too. Aunts, uncles, and grandparents are always included in holiday celebrations. During the week, most families try to eat at least one meal a day together.

Italian meals can be either casual or more formal. Formal Italian meals have several courses and may last for two hours or more. The meal starts with antipasti, or appetizers.

Antipasti may include artichoke hearts, olives, mozzarella cheese, and cold cuts such as salami. Next, a pasta dish is served. Soup or risotto may be substituted for pasta. The second course is meat, often beef, veal, pork, poultry, or fish. A side dish such as potato, salad, or a vegetable might be served. The meal ends with a dessert of fresh fruit, cheese, or pastries.

Food is also an important part of celebrating holidays. Special Easter bread called colomba is baked in dove-shaped pans (because *colomba* is the Italian word for dove) and given away as gifts. Panettone, bread stuffed with raisins and candied oranges, is baked and eaten during the Christmas season.

Panettone bread, baked with raisins and other sweet ingredients, is made and served during the Christmas season in Italy.

Climate

Italy's location close to the Mediterranean Sea gives the country a **temperate** climate. However, changes in weather conditions swing widely from northern to southern Italy. During the winter, the mountains in the north and parts of the lower Po Valley are covered in snow. In the summer, the mountains stay cool, but the valley can be hot and humid.

Central Italy receives the most rainfall during the winter but experiences dry summers. During the winter, the warmest it gets is 54 degrees Fahrenheit (12 degrees Celsius). But, summer temperatures can reach 97 °F (36 °C). Tuscany, located in central Italy, is famous for its olive trees and olive oil. The olive oil produced there is considered to be one of the finest food products in Italy. The majority of the country's olive trees grow in southern Italy, however.

The weather is slightly drier and warmer in southern Italy, the source of a popular spice called pepperoncino (pep-er-awn-CHEE-noh). The plant produces hot red chili peppers, which grow well in warm, sunny places. Pepperoncino first appeared in Italy during the time of Christopher Columbus, who reportedly brought it back from his travels in the New World.

History

People have lived in Italy for thousands of years. The first known group, the Etruscans, arrived around 1000 BCE.

A woman sells pepperoncino at her sidewalk stall.

The Etruscans established the earliest real towns in central Italy, the so-called city-states. These ancient peoples were very sophisticated and artistic. They also enjoyed eating. Murals show large banquet scenes, where Etruscan tables overflowed with such foods as tuna, deer, birds, and grapes.

An Etruscan wall painting depicts a banquet scene dating from 480–470 BCE.

The Etruscans ruled the area until 510 BCE when Rome, a powerful nearby city-state, overthrew them and established a republic. Hundreds of years later, Rome, by then a vast empire, began to weaken. German tribes saw an opportunity for invasion, and in 476 CE these central Europeans overthrew the last Roman emperor.

For almost five hundred years Italy was not united. Most people on the peninsula lived in rural areas. The remaining cities had very few occupants. Because people in the various regions were isolated from one another, they developed different ways of preparing food.

During the twelfth and thirteenth century, cities began to grow again, and the city-state form of organization reappeared. People were soon exploring art and science, and the city-states of the Italian peninsula became wealthy. Venice especially grew in wealth because of its location, at a crossroad between central Europe and the Muslim world. The **Renaissance** had begun. By 1861 the Kingdom of Italy had formed. In 1946, a year after the end of World War II, Italy became a republic.

Not only were science and art developing during the Renaissance, but so was Italian cooking. One contributor was the Venetian Marco Polo, who traveled to China. On his return, he brought unusual spices and information about new cooking techniques.

Later, tomatoes arrived from the New World via Spain. At first, people thought the strange, reddish fruit was poisonous. But in 1692 the use of tomatoes in a sauce was reported in southern Italy, where the plants were growing like weeds under the sun. Tomatoes have since become one of the most important ingredients in Italian cooking.

The art of cooking began to develop in Italy during the Renaissance.

The variety of food found in Italy is a product of its diverse people and distinctive landscapes. Throughout its rich history, Italian food has blossomed into a variety of tasty cheeses, creamy risottos, delicious pastas served with classic sauces, and much more.

TWO
Food Regions of Italy

||||||||||||||||||||||||||||||||||||||||||||||||||||||||||||||||||||||||||||||||||||||||||||||||||||||

Italy's regions are grouped into three main areas: northern, central, and southern. Because Italy's climate varies from north to south, food served in the twenty different regions varies, too. The creamy rice dish risotto is served in northern Italy, especially in the regions of Piedmont and Lombardy, where most of the country's rice is grown. Pasta with tomato sauce, made of vine-ripened tomatoes, freshly cut basil, and oregano, is eaten in central Italy in the regions of Tuscany and Lazio. The southern Italian region of Campania gave birth to a world-famous dish: pizza.

Northern Italy

Some of the most northern mountainous regions in Italy are the Aosta (O-stah) Valley, Trentino (Tren-TEE-noh)–Alto Adige (Ahl-toh AH-dee-jay), and Friuli (free-OO-lee)–Venezia Giulia (ve-NEE-tsyah JOO-lyah). The foods of Aosta Valley have Swiss and French influences. Thick stews and soups are made

THE FOOD REGIONS OF Italy

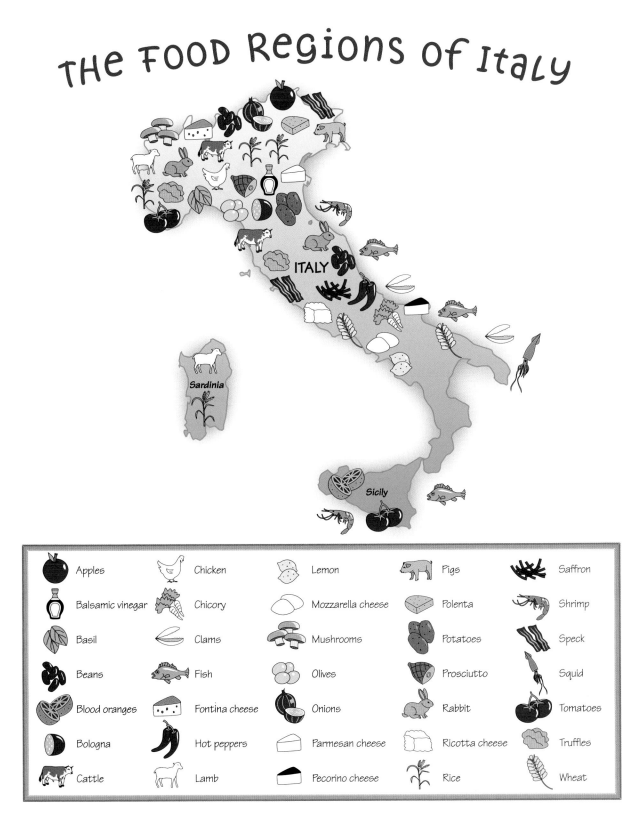

ITALY

Sardinia

Sicily

Apples	Chicken	Lemon	Pigs	Saffron
Balsamic vinegar	Chicory	Mozzarella cheese	Polenta	Shrimp
Basil	Clams	Mushrooms	Potatoes	Speck
Beans	Fish	Olives	Prosciutto	Squid
Blood oranges	Fontina cheese	Onions	Rabbit	Tomatoes
Bologna	Hot peppers	Parmesan cheese	Ricotta cheese	Truffles
Cattle	Lamb	Pecorino cheese	Rice	Wheat

from meat such as venison or beef, along with onions, beans, and vegetables. Polenta, a cornmeal dish, may be served with the stew. Cabbage soup is flavored with rich prosciutto (proh-SHOO-toh), a **cured** raw ham, and fontina cheese.

Trentino–Alto Adige borders Austria. It is so closely connected to Austria that many street signs are in German as well as Italian. Austrian dishes such as sauerkraut, knödel, and goulash, which may be made from beef, are served there. Knödel is made from stale bread, milk, eggs, calf liver or ham, and a little bit of nutmeg. These ingredients are mixed and formed into small balls like dumplings, which are poached in chicken broth and served in the cooking liquid.

Apples grow in the valleys of Trentino–Alto Adige and are used to make strudel, paper-thin layers of pastry wrapped around apple filling. In more recent years, sausage-and-apple pizza has been served in the region.

Speck, a type of ham similar to bacon, is also made in northern Italy. The ham is smoked, salted, and seasoned with black pepper, garlic, pimento, and other ingredients. Speck is often served with horseradish sauce as antipasti or eaten as a snack.

Friuli–Venezia Giulia lies in the Italian northeast and borders Austria and Hungary. Strudel and Viennese sausage are often served. But Friuli–Venezia Giulia also has customized pork products such as prosciutto, salami, and pancetta (pahn-chet-AH), a product similar to American bacon.

Polenta

A staple in the northern Italian diet is a dish called polenta. It is a cornmeal mush that can be cooked until it is firm or removed from the heat and served while it is soft and creamy. In northern Italy, polenta is cooked until it is firm enough to be sliced into thick pieces. Polenta can be eaten with meat or sweetened with cream and nutmeg for dessert. Polenta is fun to make, but be prepared to stir! An adult should help in preparing and cooking this dish.

Ingredients

4 cups water
1 cup ground yellow cornmeal
One-half stick of butter
Salt

Directions

Heat water with a couple of dashes of salt to a boil. Whisk cornmeal into the water until it is completely absorbed. Lower the heat to a simmer. Add the butter. Stir the  polenta continuously until it is firm, about 30 minutes. Add salt to taste.

Serve with stew or meat and sauce.

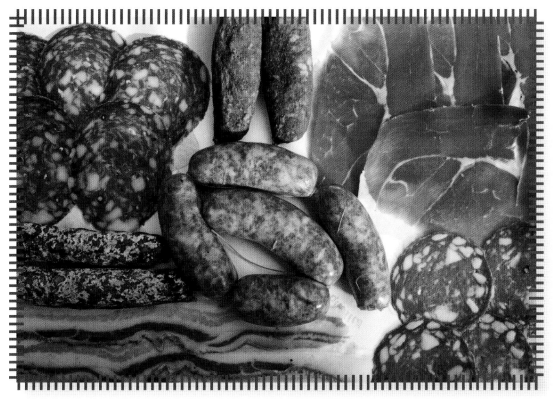

Friuli-Venezia Giulia is known for its pork products of prosciutto (top right), salami (top left and bottom right), and pancetta (bottom left).

Another region of northern Italy is Lombardy, one of the wealthier regions of the country, where food tastes are quite sophisticated. Bollito misto (buh-LEE-toh mis-TOH), or mixed boiled meats, is a local favorite. This dish has many variations, but it can contain beef, pork sausage, cow tongue, chicken, ham, and calf's head. The platter is served with a variety of sauces. Trentino–Alto Adige, Piedmont, and Veneto are among the other regions that enjoy bollito misto.

Piedmont lies in northwestern Italy, bordering France and Switzerland. In this land of lakes, valleys, and rolling hills, people often serve meat dishes such as roast beef, lamb, rabbit, or chicken simmered in local red wine. White truffles are harvested in Alba in the southern Piedmont region. These prized truffles, which look like misshapen potatoes, can sell for thousands of dollars per pound.

Liguria, which borders the Ligurian Sea, is famous for its focaccia (foh-KAH-chuh). This flatbread is usually seasoned with coarse salt and rosemary. But many other toppings can be added, such as melted cheese, onions, tomatoes, or olives.

Because Veneto borders the Adriatic Sea, a wide variety of seafood is served, including eel, sardine, shrimp, clams, and cod. This region is also the home of one of the most beautiful cities in the world, Venice. In the past, merchants from Europe and the Orient traded spices in Venice. Today, traditional Venetian dishes include calf's liver sautéed in onions and a thick soup of rice and peas.

In north central Italy, Emilia-Romagna (e-MEE-lyah roh-MAH-nyah) produces many well-known Italian foods, such as prosciutto, balsamic vinegar, and Parmesan cheese. The most delicious prosciutto in Italy,

The traditional Ligurian focaccia bread is prepared with coarse salt and rosemary.

The Land of Rice

The majority of Italy's rice is grown in Piedmont and Lombardy. Even so, rice is grown in smaller quantities elsewhere in Italy, for example, in the Emilia-Romagna and Veneto regions, and on the island of Sardinia. Italy grows more rice than any other country in the European Union. It exports over half its rice to other countries. In Italy rice is used to make risotto, a traditional northern dish. It is also used in soups and to make handheld snacks such as arancini (ah-rahn-CHEE-nee), which are stuffed rice balls. Italians prefer short- or medium-grain rice because it makes the creamiest risotto, one of the country's most popular menu items. Long-grain rice, which is served in India and Asia, is less favored.

which is cured in the province of Parma located in Emilia-Romagna, has a smooth texture and a slightly sweet, salty taste. Prosciutto goes well with melon and figs, or it can be cooked with other meat to add flavoring.

Parmigiano-Reggiano (parm-MEE-jah-noh reh-JEE-ah-noh), also known as Parmesan cheese, is made at many farms in Emilia-Romagna. The making of this cheese is very controlled. To be sure of producing high-quality raw milk for the cheese, the cows are fed on grass and hay only.

The capital city of Emilia-Romagna is Bologna (buh-lohn-yah). This is the area where mortadella di Bologna is made. Not to be

Mortadella, a product from Bologna, Italy, is made from ground pork and accented with white squares of fat.

confused with bologna from the United States, mortadella di Bologna is made with finely ground pork and a blend of fine spices. The texture is firm, and each slice is accented with white squares of fat.

One dish that is prepared in many northern areas is "hunter's wife's chicken," usually known by its Italian name: chicken cacciatore (kah-chuh-tawr-ay). This popular dish has many variations. Mushrooms, carrots, olives, onions, garlic, and parsley often are added to simmering chicken.

Central Italy

One of the most picturesque regions in central Italy is Tuscany, home of famous cities such as Florence and Pisa, as well as picturesque ancient villages. Grazing on its green, rolling hills are Chianina (kee-ah-NEE-nah) cattle. The beef from the Chianina is very flavorful. Delicious t-bone steaks are seasoned with salt, pepper, and fresh olive oil, then grilled.

On the east-central coast of Italy, Marche (mahr-KAY) is known for its rustic food. Roasted rabbit, beans, and potatoes may be found on the table. Because the area borders the sea, fish soup is sometimes served.

The town of Norcia (nor-KEE-ah), located in the Umbria region, holds a black truffle festival on the last weekend of February. Although not as expensive as white truffles, black truffles are delicious when added to pasta and risotto dishes. Norcia is also known for its raw and dried sausages. The sausage stuffing may include pine nuts, raisins, or orange peel. Throughout Umbria, wonderful sweets such as macaroons made from hazelnuts are popular.

Within the Lazio (laht-ZEE-oh) region is one of the world's most famous cities, Rome. This is also where the dish called spaghetti alla carbonara originated. There are many different stories of how this dish of bacon, eggs, and pasta came about. However, none have been proven to be true. It is certain, however, that *carbonara* means charcoal in Italian. In one version of the story, the dish was introduced to the city by peasants from Abruzzo who used to come to the city to sell charcoal.

Ricotta cheese is made from sheep, cow, or buffalo milk. Even though it can be found anywhere in Italy, the best ricotta comes from Lazio. Ricotta is often added to pasta dishes such as lasagna.

Located in the Mediterranean Sea, with the Tyrrhenian Sea separating it from the mainland of Italy, is the island of Sardinia (sar-din-EE-ah). Extinct volcanoes slope toward the turquoise

A cheesemaker prepares ricotta, a soft cheese made of sheep, cow, or buffalo milk.

waters; sheep graze throughout the hills and valleys. Lamb dishes are a local favorite, as is sheep's milk cheese. Another common food is a paper-thin, crisp flatbread, similar to a cracker, which is sprinkled with salt and rosemary. In the past, sheep herders carried this bread while away from home taking care of the sheep.

The region of Abruzzi is located in the tall mountains of the Apennines. Saffron, which grows in Abruzzi, along with hot chili peppers, are added to spice up the dishes served in the region.

Southern Italy

Right below Abruzzi, also in the Apennines, is Molise. The food in this small region is very similar to that in Abruzzi. Molise boasts such rustic local specialties as chicory, pecorino, and egg soup. Chicory is a green, bitter root, and pecorino is sheep's milk cheese. Different kinds of pecorino are made all over Italy.

Bordering the Mediterranean Sea is Campania (kahm-PAH-nyah). The Amalfi coast, one of the most beautiful in Italy, is situated here. Lemon trees in pots balanced on cliffs produce large, sweet lemons with very few seeds. One of the main cities in Campania is Naples, the home of pizza. Historians believe that this dish was introduced around 1000 CE when the word *pizza*, which means pie, began to appear in writing.

Naples, a city in southern Italy, is famous for its pizza.

Campania's Mozzarella Cheese

Most mozzarella cheese sold in the United States is made with cow's milk. This type of mozzarella is rubbery and has very little flavor. Campania mozzarella made from the milk of the water buffalo, is sold and eaten before it is two days old. This very fresh cheese has a delicate flavor and a soft, squishy texture. Caprese salad, which consists of tomatoes, basil leaves, and fresh mozzarella, is a popular dish made all over Italy (see page 41 for the recipe). For pizza, however, cheese from cow's milk is better than the kind made from the milk of water buffalo.

Even though very little rain falls on the Apulia region, its fertile plain, called Tavoliere, is covered at harvest time with wide fields of yellow, swaying wheat. Apulia's coastline takes up about three-quarters of the region. Seafood such as squid, tuna, mussels, and oysters are common dishes.

The Basilicata and Calabria regions are at the end of the Italian "boot." In the past, these southern regions were very poor.

Because of this, their dishes were and still are basic. Pasta with turnip tops is made in Basilicata. Sweet dishes are flavored with honey produced in Calabria. One such dish is turnovers filled with ricotta and pecorino cheeses and sweetened with honey. Fish is also important to these coastal regions. In addition, beans such as chickpeas and fava beans are served.

On Sicily, volcanic ash from Mount Etna has made the soil very fertile. A variety of fruits and vegetables grow on the island. The blood orange has dark red pulp and a taste similar to that of sweet berries. Sicily produces the sweetest blood oranges in Italy, as well as fragrant lemons and juicy mandarin oranges.

Natural food seasonings are also found on Sicily. Growing close to the ground are caper plants. The small flower buds are picked, pickled, and sprinkled on dishes for flavoring. On the northwest coast of Sicily, sea salt is harvested from natural salt pans.

Because Sicily is surrounded by the sea, fishing is very important. Fresh swordfish, tuna, octopus, mussels, and clams can be bought at the island's many fish markets.

The catch of the day is on sale at a fish market in Marsala, Sicily.

Pepperoncino and Southern Italy

In the past, southern Italy was poorer than the rest of Italy. To spice up bland dishes, the chili pepper pepperoncino, locally known as "little devil," was added.

The best pepperoncino in Italy is grown in Basilicata and Calabria. Today, a shaker jar of these dried reddish flakes can be found in any pizzeria on Earth.

Popular Italian dishes are served around the world. However, the various regions of Italy have created dishes of many types, all of them featuring the creative use of local ingredients.

THREE
Daily Life

|||||||||||||||||||||||||||||||||||||||||||||||||||||||||||||||||||||||||||||||||||||||||

Italian families are close-knit. Many Italian families consider this relationship to be the most important one in life. It is not uncommon for family members to work together in business. For example, the Barilla family has been in the pasta business for almost 130 years. From its base in Parma, a province in Emilia-Romagna, Barilla has become the largest pasta manufacturer in the world, producing four thousand tons of pasta each day.

Most Italian families, about two-thirds, live in cities. The rest live in rural villages. In 2009 the population of Italy was more than 58 million. The mountainous areas of Italy, the Alps and the Apennines, have the fewest people. The largest city in Italy is Rome, with a population of more than 2.5 million people. The next two largest cities are Milan in the north, with more than 1.2 million people, and Naples in the south, with just over a million people.

The two most populated regions are Lombardy and Liguria, in the north, boasting more than one major manufacturing industry. Milan, located in Lombardy, is the fashion capital of the world. Steel and shipbuilding industries can be found in Liguria.

Liguria is also well known because of its basil pesto, a popular Italian sauce created in the Ligurian city of Genoa. This thick, green paste contains basil, Parmesan and pecorino cheeses, and olive oil, along with garlic, pine nuts, and salt. Pesto is poured on top of pasta and spread on bread. It is also added to soups and vegetables to give them a savory flavor.

The Campania region in the south, anchored by Naples, is also highly populated. It is said that the air in Naples smells of pizza. Neapolitan pizza, which is served with tomato sauce seasoned with basil, along with olive oil and fresh mozzarella, is fed to children at a very young age. The habit of eating pizza continues into old age.

Shopping for Food

In the past, Italians shopped daily and bought all their food fresh from small markets. Today, because more women are working, less time is available for grocery shopping. So having all food products in one location, such as a supermarket, is a convenient setup.

The stocking of supermarket shelves requires food to be brought in from warehouses and local markets and unloaded. Usually the food is transported by huge trucks, as in the United States. Venice, however, has canals instead of roads. In this unique situation, all supermarket goods are transported by boat.

Even though supermarkets are popular, Italians prefer to shop daily to get the freshest ingredients. Time permitting, they may

Pizza is a common treat for all in the city of Naples.

visit the local bakery for bread or rolls, then go to a deli for lunch meat, sausage, and cheese. Beef, pork, and chicken are purchased from a butcher. Crab, fish, squid, and other seafood delicacies are bought at the fish market or sometimes obtained fresh off the boat. Produce markets sell fruits and vegetables.

Another source for groceries is local farmers markets, where fresh produce, cheese, and meat are displayed in the stalls of individual farmers. Some stalls have been managed by the same family for many generations. One historic marketplace is Campo de Fiori market in Rome, where scores of stalls are set up in a public square or piazza (pee-AH-zuh). Some farmers sell ready-made

For the most fresh farm products, many Italians head to the Campo de Fiori market in Rome.

snacks, such as cheese pizza by the slice or homemade soup by the bowl. In addition, the market is surrounded by cafés, where shoppers can enjoy both eating and people watching.

Home Life

Italians live very differently according to whether they are in a city or in a rural area. City families live in apartments, which they buy rather than rent. When children grow up and move out, they usually live close to their parents. It is not uncommon for grandparents to babysit when young mothers go to work. Grandparents may also help with the shopping and cooking. In big cities, where grandparents may not be available for baby-sitting, day-care centers, previously rare in Italy, have become less unusual.

More and more Italian women are working outside the home, and families are smaller than they used to be. Today, most couples have only one or two children. Yet in Italy as elsewhere, working women also have to cook and clean at home. In the interest of serving healthy meals without spending hours on shopping and preparation, Italian households are buying more and more frozen food.

The average city apartment size is about 1,000 to 1,200 square feet (93–111 square meters). Kitchens are compact and efficient. Electricity is very expensive, but almost every household has modern conveniences. In northern and central Italy the standard of living is higher than southern Italy.

Italian villages now offer apartment living, but rural areas are still dotted with farms. The majority are small family farms, consisting of about 12 acres (5 hectares), on which the people grow crops or raise livestock. Some traditional family farms still use older farming methods. The larger commercial farms have become modernized, however. Besides grapes and olives, Italian farmers may grow artichokes, sugar beets, cherries, peaches, pears, tomatoes, barley, corn, or rice. The most common livestock animals are pigs, chickens, sheep, and cattle. Even so, meat must be imported from other countries because Italians eat so much of it.

Italians and Eating

Italians love food. They use it to establish and create relationships with family and friends. When visiting an Italian home, it is customary for Italians to offer visitors a drink or food. Cheese is a favorite snack, and a variety of cheeses, such as gorgonzola, provolone, mozzarella, fontina, and asiago, are served alone or with other dishes.

Italians typically eat three meals a day: breakfast, lunch, and dinner. Breakfast is the lightest meal. It is usually a cup of coffee, **espresso**, or **cappuccino**, with sweet breads or rolls. Fruit and juice may also be served.

In the past, people ate their main meal, consisting of several courses, at midday and then took a nap. Dinner was a lighter meal, mainly leftovers. However, in modern times, schedules have changed. Today, many families eat the larger meal in the evening because there is no time for long afternoon naps.

Pasta

The national food of Italy is pasta. This simple carbohydrate is made out of flour and water and sometimes eggs. In the past, pasta was eaten every day in most of the country. But today,

Italy and Its Wine

Italy is one of the top wine-producing countries in the world. Growing grapes is very important. Vineyards are planted from northern regions all the way to southern Italy.

Wine is always on the table at lunch and dinner. Even children drink wine, which the parents dilute by adding water. Because Italians drink wine from an early age, they generally drink it in moderation throughout their lives.

like health-conscious people everywhere, Italians try to limit the amount of carbohydrates they eat.

Pasta comes in many sizes and shapes, such as bows, called farfalle, and small tubes, such as ziti. But the most common type of pasta is long noodles. The thinnest noodle is 1/16 inch thick and is called capellini, or angel hair. Spaghetti and linguine have the same thickness: 1/8 inch. The two forms of pasta are different, though, because spaghetti is round and linguine is flat. Fettuccine is also flat but is a bit wider, at 1/4 inch. The widest pasta, at 1 inch, is called pappardelle.

Italy is famous for its pasta. It comes in many shapes and sizes, but one of the most familiar is spaghetti.

Different types of pasta are served in different regions of Italy. Ravioli, small squares of dough filled with ground meat, can be found in northern Italy. Lasagna, wide noodles baked with cheese and meat sauce, and tortellini, pasta shaped like a ring stuffed with meat, are served in Bologna. Cannelloni, large tube-shaped pasta, often stuffed with cheese, is found in Sicily. Spaghetti with tomato or clam sauce is served in Naples. Northern Italians eat less pasta than the rest of Italy. Instead, they eat risotto, prepared in a variety of ways, or polenta. Butter is used more in the north, where pasta with a cream sauce is common. Olive oil is used more in the south.

Common Kitchen Ingredients

Having cooking skills is very important to Italian women, and girls help in the kitchen from an early age. Each kitchen must have basic ingredients, and girls soon learn that olive oil is one of the most important. Italians are very particular about their olive oil, which they judge on the basis of quality and flavor. Olive oil can be drizzled on salads and vegetables or used to sauté or deep-fry vegetables. It is also used to preserve mushrooms, garlic cloves, tomatoes, and artichoke hearts, especially in southern Italy.

Herbs found in an Italian kitchen include rosemary, thyme, bay leaf, sage, mint, and parsley. Some herbs are served more in various regions. Mint is used in dishes served in the Lazio region, where Rome is located. Marjoram, similar to oregano, is used in the Liguria region of northwestern Italy.

Two of the most common herbs in Italian cooking are basil and oregano. Many Italians grow basil in their homes to be sure of a fresh supply of the herb. Oregano is picked and dried. It is then used to season fish, eggplant, soups, and sauces.

Eating Out

In Italy, cafés, pizzerias, trattorias, and osterias are favorite places for meeting friends and socializing. Owners of cafés,

Italian Sausages

Sausages are an important part of the food culture in Italy. Italian sausages are usually made from pork. But, other meat such as goose or donkey may be used, depending on the region. Sausages are made by combining ground meat with spices and stuffing the mixture into thin natural casings. Italian sausages are sold in three different forms: raw, aged or dried, and cooked. Sausages sold raw can be either cooked on a grill in the casing or removed from the casing, fried, and served with pasta. Aged or dried sausage is sliced thin and served on antipasto platters. Cooked sausage is simply reheated.

which serve drinks and snacks, encourage their customers to stay. In the spring, Italians sit for hours reading, writing, or socializing with friends in outdoor cafés. At trattorias and osterias, friends and family will stay late into the night drinking wine after a good meal. Sunday afternoon is a favorite time for Italian families to eat out.

Caprese Salad

Authentic caprese salads have a distinctive taste because they are made with fresh water buffalo mozzarella. If you can, look for this type of mozzarella in a specialty store. Have an adult help you with the slicing.

Ingredients

1 large red tomato, sliced
1 bunch fresh basil leaves with the stems removed
1/4 pound fresh mozzarella, sliced
Olive oil
Salt

Directions

Arrange the tomato slices in a circle. Place one or two basil leaves on top of each tomato slice. Place equal amounts of sliced mozzarella on top of each tomato slice. Drizzle olive oil on top. Sprinkle with salt.

Teens enjoy gelato in Rome.

To find coffee, ice cream, alcohol, pastries, and other snacks in Italy, people go to a bar, where they eat or drink standing next to a high counter. Customers must pay extra to sit at a table.

Another common sight in almost every Italian town is the gelateria, the source of the treat called gelato. Similar to ice cream but lighter because it's made with more milk than cream, gelato is stored at a slightly warmer temperature than ice cream. It comes in many flavors, including chocolate, pistachio, strawberry, and coconut.

FOUR

Festivals and Traditions

||||||||||||||||||||||||||||||||||||||||||||||||||||||||||||||||||||||||||||||||||||||||||||

It is said that there's a festival or holiday on almost every day in Italy. There are food festivals for grapes, truffles, artichokes, and more. But the most important celebrations and holidays have a basis in religion. Ninety-five percent—almost the entire population—of Italy is Roman Catholic.

Religious Festivals

One of the most common celebrations in Italy is Saint's Day. In the Middle Ages, every small town, village, and city was assigned a saint by the Catholic Church. This saint became a symbol for the residents, and they prayed to him or her for help or guidance. Saint's Day is celebrated differently in each town, but food is always part of the festivities.

Saint Joseph's Day, celebrated on March 19, honors the saint who is believed to have stopped a severe famine in Sicily in the Middle Ages. The famine was due to a drought, and the Sicilians prayed to God for rain. They also asked Saint Joseph to intercede with God on their behalf. Finally, the rain came and the crops grew. After the harvest, there was a great feast to honor Saint Joseph. Huge tables were loaded down with breads, cakes, and pastries, as well as stuffed artichoke hearts, fava beans, fish dishes, and pasta. Poor people were fed, as well as those who had contributed food to the feast, a custom that continues to this day.

Celebrated on November 1 throughout Italy is All Saints Day. The next day, called All Souls Day, is a time to remember loved ones who have passed away. Dishes made with peas or lentils are served. Traditionally, food and drink are left for relatives who have died.

The origin of the Palio, or annual horse race festival held in the Tuscan city of Siena, has been lost over time. Its dates, however, are closely related to religious traditions. The first leg of this race takes place on July 2, the day of the Catholic festival called the Feast of the Visitation. This day celebrates the visit of the Virgin Mary to her cousin Elizabeth, some months before the birth of Jesus. The second leg of the race, on August 16, comes one day after the Feast of the Assumption. This feast commemorates the death of the Virgin Mary and her ascension into heaven.

The night before the race, each contrada, or subdivision of Siena, hosts a dinner. Fifty-foot-long tables are set up on cobblestoned streets. Meat, pasta, and vegetables are passed down the tables on large platters.

The next day, each horse is blessed at the local church. Then begins a beautiful, hours-long pageant. The race, which is over

Beans of the Dead: Cookies for All Souls Day

The traditional dessert for the meal on All Soul's Day consists of sweet, almond-flavored cookies called "beans of the dead" or, sometimes, "bones of the dead." An adult should help in preparing and baking.

Ingredients

1 cup flour

1 cup confectioners' sugar

2 teaspoons baking powder

3/4 teaspoon ground cloves

2 beaten eggs

1 teaspoon almond extract

Directions

Stir flour, sugar, baking powder, and cloves in a bowl. Add the beaten eggs and almond extract; mix well. Cover with a clean dish towel and let dough rise overnight.

Preheat the oven to 325 degrees Fahrenheit. Break dough into half-inch balls and form into curved shapes to look like kidney beans. Place on a greased cookie sheet. Bake the cookies for 10 to 15 minutes, until slightly brown.

The evening before the Palio celebration in Siena, festivalgoers feast at long tables on meat, pasta, and vegetable dishes.

very quickly, is then held in the main square, the Piazza del Campo.

Another popular celebration is Carnival Day. Like Mardi Gras in New Orleans, Carnival Day is the day before Ash Wednesday, the beginning of Lent. Lent is a period of fasting and repenting observed by many Christians; it is especially important in the Catholic Church. Carnival is traditional in many parts of Italy, but Venice has the largest celebration. People dress in elaborate costumes and wear masks. Music is played in the streets.

Before Lent, a period of fasting, Carnival Day is celebrated in Venice, where traditionally many wear masks and fancy costumes.

Children throw confetti, and shopkeepers give them snacks, such as small balls of fried dough rolled in powdered sugar, or sweet pasta that has been fried and sprinkled with sugar or drizzled with honey.

Easter is one of the most important holidays in Italy, second only to Christmas. In Florence, Easter is celebrated by igniting a cart filled with fireworks. There are a variety of dishes served on Easter. Roasted lamb is a favorite meat. Also, frittatas, similar to omelets, are common. There are no chocolate bunnies as in the United States, but there are chocolate eggs, made big or small, with a gift hidden inside.

Italy's Most Important Holiday

Christmas, which is celebrated from December 24 through January 6, is Italy's most important holiday. Starting early in December, street vendors sell roasted chestnuts. Colorful lights twinkle during the cold winter nights. On Christmas Eve, it is traditional for families to eat a meatless meal, such as ravioli stuffed with pumpkin. However, families in southern Italy may serve a seven-fish dinner, perhaps including salted cod, crab, sea bass, and shrimp. In Venice, roasted eel is a popular meal for Christmas Eve. In some towns, carolers roam the streets, and people visit live **nativity** scenes and attend midnight mass.

Some Italian children open their presents on Christmas Day

because Babbo Natale, or Santa Claus, is becoming a more common Christmas figure. But in other families they must wait until January 6, the day that La Befana, the good witch, traditionally brings gifts to children in Italy. According to legend, La Befana got lost trying to follow the three wise men to the manger. She, too, had been bringing gifts for Jesus. Upon realizing that she was not going to find him, however, she handed out her presents to the children she saw on her way. La Befana has been handing out presents to children ever since.

Regardless of whether Italian children receive their presents on December 25 or January 6, Christmas Day is the day for stockings. Children who were good during the year receive stockings filled with small gifts and treats. The stockings of children who were bad may be filled with black sugar, symbolizing coal.

Christmas is a day of feasting. Dishes such as tortellini, stuffed pig's foot, lamb, mashed potatoes, and lentils may be served. Pandoro, a rich, buttery cake is a favorite.

Nonreligious Festivals

Because food is such an important part of Italian culture, food festivals are held throughout the year, either to celebrate the harvest or to promote the eating of different foods within the country.

During the fall, truffles are celebrated, especially in the regions of Piedmont, Tuscany, and Marche. At one of the largest truffle festivals, held in the Piedmont city of Alba, white truffles are auctioned to chefs from around the world. In addition, a white truffle market is open for other visitors. Italy is the main European producer of prized white truffles.

A variety of fruit festivals are held across Italy. The Lazio region hosts a strawberry festival, in the town of Nemi, and a maraschino cherry festival in the town of Celleno. Maraschino cherries are made by adding a liqueur called maraschino to local, sour, Marasca cherries. In the town of Monterosso al Mare in the Liguria region, the entire population joins in the lemon festival. The streets are decorated with a lemon theme, and there is a competition to find the largest lemon.

Not only is fruit celebrated, but so are chocolate, pizza, and almonds. The chocolate festival is in October in the town of Perugia in the Umbria region. For eight days and nights, chocolate lovers gather to eat chocolate, listen to music, and dance. The Pizzafest is held in Naples every September. More than thirty stalls serve pizza with fresh tomato sauce. Cheese tasting and voting for the best pizza are just some of the activities. Almonds, which are crushed into a delicious paste called marzipan, are honored in the Sicilian city of Agrigento. At the almond blossom festival, held on the first Sunday in February, people dance and hold parades to celebrate not only the blossoms but also the coming of spring.

There are many festivals for different types of food in Italy, but one is all about eating. This huge feast, called La Panarda, is held in the Abruzzo region. Up to fifty dishes may be served,

Strawberries have their own festival during the month of June in Lazio.

such as pasta flavored with tomatoes and goose, ravioli stuffed with cinnamon and sugar, spicy pork roast, and cheese pudding. La Panarda continues all night in the village or town hosting the festival.

Overall, Italy is a place of celebration. Italians celebrate food, family, religion, and life.

FIVE

Health and Nutrition

||||||||||||||||||||||||||||||||||||||||||||||||||||||||||||||||||||||||||||||||||||||

One characteristic common to all Italian food is the use of fresh, healthful ingredients. There are many small farmers in Italy who grow their own produce and raise their own livestock. Most of Italy's produce is grown organically, without commercial **pesticides**. In addition, some of the livestock—cows, goats, pigs, and sheep—are free to roam. Such free-range animals feed on grass and other natural sources of nutrition. Italy's livestock is also free of other modern additives such as hormones.

Fish are caught in the four seas surrounding Italy plus in the country's many lakes. In all coastal towns and cities, fresh fish can be purchased right at the dock. This is good news to those who know that a diet high in fish has been proven to reduce heart disease.

Healthy Nutrition

Throughout Italy, the dishes served are varied. However, some ingredients are commonly found in kitchens from north to south.

Minestrone Soup

Overall, it is the Italians' love of local ingredients that leads to healthy habits. One classic example of a healthy traditional food is minestrone. This soup is eaten everywhere in Italy. Mostly, it consists of a variety of vegetables. However, cooks in some locations add protein in the form of chicken, ham, or pancetta. Have an adult help you prepare this tasty soup.

Ingredients

Olive oil

1/2 cup minced onion

1/4 cup chopped green beans

1/4 cup diced zucchini

1/4 cup shredded carrots

1/4 cup chopped celery

2 cloves garlic, minced

2 cups vegetable broth

1 15 oz can tomatoes, diced

1 15 oz can kidney beans, drained

1 15 oz can white beans, drained

1 tablespoon minced fresh parsley

3/4 teaspoon dried oregano

3/4 teaspoon salt

1/4 teaspoon black pepper

1/4 teaspoon dried basil

1/8 teaspoon dried thyme

1 1/2 cups hot water

2 cups fresh baby spinach

1/4 cup small shell pasta

Grated Parmesan cheese

Directions

Heat about 1 1/2 tablespoons of olive oil in a soup pot. Put in onion, green beans, zucchini, carrots, celery, and garlic and sauté for about 5 minutes. Pour in vegetable broth, drained tomatoes and beans, and hot water. Add parsley, oregano, salt, black pepper, basil, and thyme. Bring to a boil. Turn the heat down until soup is simmering. Let it simmer for 20 minutes. Add spinach leaves and pasta. Cook for an additional 20 minutes. When serving, sprinkle Parmesan cheese over the top.

These ingredients are extra-virgin olive oil, wine, cheese, tomatoes, and pasta. Each one has definite health benefits.

Extra-virgin olive oil is a vegetable fat that can be used right after it has been extracted from olives. Because of its freshness, extra-virgin olive oil helps reduce the risk of heart disease. It also is thought to guard against some cancers.

Because Italians tend not to drink wine in excess, they benefit from a recently discovered effect of consumption: wine taken in moderation can help reduce heart disease. Red wine also has

Ingredients such as extra-virgin olive oil, wine, cheese, pasta, and vegetables contribute to the good health of many Italians.

been shown to cut back on the growth of some potentially cancer-causing tumors.

A variety of cheeses can be found in every region of Italy. The habit of eating cheese as dessert, with fruit, or as a snack has helped Italians in many ways. Cheese fortifies their diet by providing important minerals and vitamins, including calcium, vitamin A, and vitamin B12. Calcium promotes the development of strong bones. Vitamin A helps with vision and in keeping skin healthy. Vitamin B12 is important in maintaining the health of nerve cells. Cheese also protects teeth from cavities.

Italians love mushrooms, which they both harvest in the wild and buy in stores and from markets. Mushrooms are served in soup, risotto, and pasta. This vegetable is packed with minerals such as potassium, zinc, and several B vitamins.

Tomatoes, fresh and canned, are found in many regional Italian dishes. This fruit has lots of vitamin C, which is believed to help prevent colds and fight eye disease. Tomatoes also prevent some cancers and heart disease.

Eating pasta is also another healthy Italian habit. The average Italian consumes about 60 pounds of pasta per year. Some families make their pasta at home, but the majority of Italians purchase it in dry form, ready to cook. Pasta is a complex carbohydrate, meaning that it releases energy into the body slowly. Athletes such as runners and bicyclists eat a lot of complex carbohydrates because this diet helps them go long distances before getting tired.

Pasta, a favorite of many Italians, is a product with health benefits such as the slow release of energy.

Italians healthy eating habits in the past have made them less likely to die of heart disease. They are also less likely to be obese. This is an advantage because obesity is known to lead to many health complications. Because of their healthy lifestyle, Italians have a long life expectancy. Many live to be eighty years old.

However, obesity is becoming a problem with Italian children. Departures from the traditional diet in favor of junk food and soft drinks are to blame, as well as inactivity. Parents are becoming more aware of the problem and are cutting back on the amount of unhealthy food their children consume. In addition, cities are building new parks to encourage children to exercise outdoors.

Food, the Italian Way

Throughout history, Italians have used their imagination to create delicious and nutritious dishes: hearty stews, steaming pastas, decorative desserts, and many more. The people's passion for life shines through in their food. Some of the most loved in the world comes from Italy.

Glossary

archipelago   group of small islands

cappuccino   espresso mixed with steamed milk

cured   preserved by salting

espresso   a strong coffee made from dark coffee beans

mural   large painted picture on a wall

nativity   the birth of Jesus

osteria   a simple tavern found in a country setting

pesticide   a poison used to kill weeds and bugs

Renaissance   the rebirth of learning and art that took place in Europe from the fourteenth to the sixteenth century

savory   describing a flavor that is noticeable but not sweet

temperate   neither too hot nor too cold

trattoria   an eating establishment that is less formal than a restaurant

Find Out More

BOOKS

Gioffre, Rosalba. *Fun with Italian Cooking*. New York: PowerKids Press, 2009.

Goodman, Polly. *Italy* (Food Around the World). London: Hodder Wayland, 2010.

Locricchio, Matthew. *The Cooking of Italy*. New York: Marshall Cavendish Benchmark, 2012.

DVD

Italian Cuisine. Bravo Chef, 2009.

WEBSITES

Italian History

www.kidspast.com/world-history/0289-the-renaissance-italy.php

The Renaissance section of this site allows the student to browse through Italian history, with a detour to the English Renaissance. Colorful pictures and interesting text make it easy to learn about this important period.

Italian Language

www.wisitalia.org/pages/ItalianWebs.html

Students can learn Italian through this site from online courses and podcasts.

Visual Geography Series

http://vgsbooks.com/

To access this site's information about the land of Italy, its government, cultural life, and economy, just select "Italy" from the list of links on the left. The site can be used by students and teachers alike to get in-depth information ranging from the gory side of gladiators' combat to relations between the United States and Italy.

Index

Page numbers in **boldface** are illustrations and charts.

About the Author

Sara Louise Kras has written twenty-nine books for children. She has traveled around the world visiting many countries. While in Italy, she climbed the Tower of Pisa, walked through the Roman Forum, and took pictures of the Coliseum. She explored the waterways of Venice. The caprese salad was Kras's favorite food while she was in Italy, but she also enjoyed many of the country's pasta dishes. She currently lives in Glendale, California, with her husband and cat.